How to Manage a Family Run Business

A Step by Step Guide To Managing a Family Owned Business

By Meir Liraz

(Including 10 Special Bonuses)

Published by Liraz Publishing

www.BizMove.com

Copyright © Liraz Publishing. All rights reserved.

ISBN: 9781695823051

Table of Contents

1. Essentials of Family Run Business Management ... 5
2. Understanding The Family Business ... 19
3. How to Balance Family And Business Goals ... 32
4. Common Problems in Managing a Family Business and How to solve Them ... 41
5. How to Choose a Successor ... 56
6. Family Run Business Assessment ... 72
7. Family Business Strategic Plan ... 75
8. How to Improve Your Leadership Skills ... 77
Appendix: Special Free Bonuses ... 92

MEIR LIRAZ

1. Essentials of Family Run Business Management

No small business is easy to manage, and this is especially true in a family business. It is subject to all the problems that beset small companies plus those that can, and often do, arise when relatives try to work together.

The family member who is charged with managing the family business company has to work at initiating and maintaining sound management practices. By describing what is to be done and under what circumstances such practices help prevent some of the confusion and conflicts that may be perpetuated by self centered family members. Such relatives sometimes regard the company as existing primarily to satisfy their desires.

The questions in this checklist are designed to help chief executive officers to review the management practices of their small family companies. The comments that follow each question are intended to stimulate thought rather than to include the many and various aspects suggested by the question.

Is executive time used on high priority tasks?

The time of the owner-manager is one of the most valuable assets of a small business. It should not be dribbled away in routine tasks that can be done as well, if not better, by other employees. Never lose sight of the fact that you as owner/manager, have to make the judgments that will determine the success of your business. You may want to run a check on how your time is used. You can do so by keeping a log for the next several weeks. On a calendar memorandum pad jot down what you do in half hour or hour blocks. Then review your notes against the questions: Was my time spent on management tasks such as reviewing last week's sales figures and noting areas for improvement? Or did I let it dribble away on routine tasks such as opening the mail and sorting bills of lading? You may want to ask your key personnel to run the same sort of check on their time.

Do you set goals and objectives?

Goals and objectives help a small company to keep headed toward profit. Goals and objectives should be specific and realistic. In addition they should be measurable, time phased, and written. List your goals and objectives by writing them out for your present successful operations. Objectives that are written out in straight-forward language provide a basis for actions by your key personnel. For example, state that you will sell certain number of units this year rather than saying you will increase sales.

Do you have written policies?

Flag this question and return to it later. Working through this checklist should suggest changes that may be needed if you have written policies. By the same token, your business will provide input for writing out policies if there are none in writing.

Is planning done to achieve these goals and objectives?

In a sense, planning is forecasting. An objective, for example, for next year might be to increase your net profit after taxes. To plan for it you need to forecast sales volume, production of finished goods inventory, raw materials requirements, and all the other elements connected with producing your forecasts, you will want to make provision for watching costs, including selling expenses. If there are key employees who can provide input into the planning, ask them to become involved in that process

Do you test or check the reality of your goals and plans with others?

Outside advisors may spot "bugs" that you and your people did not catch in the press of working through the details of goal setting and planning.

Are operations reviewed on a regular basis with the objective of reducing costs?

Costs must be kept in line for a profitable operation. Review operations periodically such as weekly or monthly, to insure that overtime is not excessive, for example. And what about quality product acceptance by customers? Costs may be excessive because of obsolete methods or machinery that has seen its best days. And what about plant layout or materials flow? Can changes be made that will save time and materials? Determine the frequency of your reviews for the various types of operations and place a tickler on your calendar to remind you of these review dates.

Are products reviewed regularly with the objective of improving them?

Products that your customers benefit from are the key to repeat sales. A regular review of your products help to keep them up to the expectation of customers. Feedback from customers can be useful here. To reduce costs sometimes a product can be modified without sacrificing use and quality. If product obsolescence is a hazard, what plans are being made to substitute new products as existing ones become obsolete?

Do you ask outside advisors for their opinion and suggestions on products and operation procedures?

Outside persons, such as friends in non-competing lines of business and management personnel from local colleges and universities can help you see the facts about your products and operating procedures. They can provide a fresh viewpoint - the viewpoint of persons who are not so involved in the products and operations as you and your key personnel. The suggestions and counsel from a local management consultant may provide benefits far in excess of his or her cost. In this area some small companies set up a board of directors to satisfy the law concerning small corporations. But that is the end of it. Members of the board are not used for their knowledge and skill in business. They can make valuable contributions and the owner/manager should use all possible opportunities for getting such concerned opinions about the various phases of the company.

Are marketing and distribution policies and procedures reviewed periodically?

The best made product in the world can run into trouble if marketing and distribution policies and procedures are not right for it. Periodical checks can help you to be aware of changes that may be taking place in the channels through which you distribute. One approach is to check your competition; does it seem to be changing channels and policies? Can you still meet the requirements of your customers by using your traditional channels of distribution?

Are there periodic reviews of profit and loss statements and other financial reports?

In these reviews you can compare your operating ratios to those for your industry. It is also helpful to review your cash flow projections to see what, if any, changes are needed in your financial planning.

Do you have an organization chart?

You may need only a simple organization chart to show accountability and to establish a chain of command. In a family business, accountability and chain of command should be spelled out so that the one who is the chief executive of the company has the "mandate" he or she needs for managing.

Do you use job descriptions for your key personnel?

When you and your key personnel write descriptions for their jobs, you and they have a clear understanding of what is to be done and by whom. Such an understanding is essential in any small business but especially critical when relatives are involved. Spelling out duties may not prevent conflicts between you and an in-law, but such detail can help you resolve misunderstandings, if and when, they occur. In addition, when, and if, a key person leaves, the job description is a helpful tool in recruiting and training a replacement.

Do you periodically compare performance of key personnel with their job descriptions?

Periodical comparison of performance helps your key personnel to be efficient. It also helps to pinpoint weak spots for you and them to work on for improvement.

Do you provide opportunities for key personnel to grow?

Your aim should be to help key personnel stay alert to new and more efficient ways to do things. Conferences, seminars, and workshops which trade associations and agencies sponsor can help key personnel to grow in their management skills and outlook. Rotating job assignments is a way to make key personnel aware of the problems that their counterparts face. Include in your budget an amount that can be spent during the year for personnel training and education.

Do you face the issue when key personnel stop growing?

Some owner-managers try to avoid the unpleasant task of facing the fact that a key person has stopped growing. It may be the result of not matching personnel and the job. Or in some family businesses, the cousin or brother-in-law never was interested in personal growth or any aspects of management. If there is little or nothing you can do about such a mismatch, face it and don't waste time trying to do the impossible. On the other hand outside problems may be crowding in on the key person. Once you know why he or she stopped growing, you can determine what needs to be done. In some cases, additional training is the answer. In other cases, the motivation that results from broadened job responsibilities resolves the problem.

Are there policies and plans for motivating employees?

Working through others is but no means an easy task. First of all, people are not puppets that can be moved by strings. Life may be a stage, as the poet said, but most people in small business are reluctant to submit to directors. Look for ways - good communications, respect for their viewpoint, incentive pay, and so on - to encourage people to want to do what you need them to do as employees in your company.

Do you have adequate employee benefit plans?

This includes life and health insurance, major medical, and pension. Benefit plans often are necessary to meet competition for skilled employees. Substantial plans can help to hold non-family key individuals in a family-owned business.

Do you have key personnel insurance on yourself and is your family protected against your untimely passing?

If these precautions are not taken, your death could result in the rapid dissolution of the business.

Is there lack of communication among key personnel?

The routine passing of information among you and your key personnel may be all that you want it to be. But what about disagreement? Do key personnel refrain from expressing disagreement with you? Good communications should provide a forum for exchanging ideas and for airing differences of opinion. Possibly an early morning meeting once a week among you and your key personnel would provide a forum for exchanging ideas.

Does your record keeping system present a realistic picture of your business? Is this the same type of record keeping system that other companies in your industry commonly use?

Appropriate records should give the owner/manager answers to questions such as: Is there sufficient cash to operate the business? To pay back the bank? To pay taxes? Is too much capital tied up in inventory? Are accounts receivable being collected promptly? Bankers and other lenders need a realistic picture. Corporate records, if your company is a corporation, should be up-to-date including corporate minutes and record books. In checking out your record keeping, keep in mind that a poor system can result in excessive and meaningless information.

Do you seek legal and financial advice on major transactions?

The fine print in contracts causes trouble for some small business owners. They did not realize until it was too late what they had agreed to do. Legal and financial advice at the appropriate time can help the owner-manager to comprehend the full scope of your company's contractual obligations and allow you to make decisions based on facts rather than assumptions. Whenever possible use your standardized contract in making contractual obligations.

Do you document informal agreements with customers, suppliers and others?

"He's as good as his word," is a fine attitude to have about customers, suppliers, and others with whom you work on a daily basis. But think for a moment; in being as "good as your word," how often do you forget? Memory slips. A note to yourself, or to a supplier to confirm a telephone conversation, for example, helps both of you to recall what you agreed, or did not agree, upon and prevents misunderstanding and hard feeling. Keep dated copies of all correspondence you send out. At some later period these copies could be invaluable.

Do you plan your major financial decisions with the help of your accountant, Lawyer, and other tax advisors?

An owner-manager cannot ignore the impact of

income taxes, as well as other taxes, on your business. You should plan major financial decisions with the help of an accountant, lawyer, and other tax advisers.

Do your plans include self development projects for yourself?

Sometimes an owner-manager sets up training for everyone in the company except him or herself. Because conditions change so rapidly you should set aside some time for activities that will help you to keep abreast of your industry and the economic world in which your company operates. Your trade association should be a source about meetings, conferences and seminars which you can use in such a program for yourself.

Are there plans for succession in the event of the untimely death of the family member who manages the company?

The successor may not be the same person who substitutes when the chief executive officer is sick or on vacation. Whether the successor is a family member or a non-family employee, the business should make the transition smoother when the family agrees upon a successor ahead of time. Such agreement is necessary if the business is to bear the expense of grooming the successor.

2. Understanding The Family Business

Family owned businesses are a vital force in the economy. more than 60 percent of all businesses are family owned or controlled. They range in size from the traditional small business to a third of the Fortune 500 firms. It is estimated that family businesses generate about half of the country's Gross National Product and half of the total wages paid.

Our economy depends heavily on the continuity and success of the family owned businesses. It is unfortunate, even alarming, that such a vital force has such a poor survival rate. Less than one third of family businesses survive the transition from first to second generation ownership. Of those that do, about half do not survive the transition from second to third generation ownership.

At any given time, 40 percent of businesses are facing the transfer of ownership issue. Founders are trying to decide what to do with their businesses; however, the options are few. The following is a list of options to consider:

Close the doors.

Sell to an outsider or employee.

Retain ownership but hire outside management.

Retain family ownership and management control.

To be one of the few family businesses that survive transfer of ownership requires a good understanding of your business and your family. There are four basic reasons why family firms fail to transfer the business from generation to generation successfully:

Lack of viability of the business.

Lack of planning.

Little desire on the owner's part to transfer the firm.

Reluctance of offspring to join the firm.

These factors, alone or in combination, make transferring a family business difficult, if not impossible. The primary cause for failure, however, is the lack of planning. With the right plans in place, the business, in most cases, will remain healthy. There are four plans that make up the transition process. By implementing these plans, you will virtually ensure the successful transfer of your business within the family hierarchy.

A brief explanation of each plan follows.

- A strategic plan for the business will allow each generation an opportunity to chart a course for the firm. Setting business goals as a family will ensure that everyone has a clear picture of the company's future.

- The family strategic plan is needed to maintain a healthy, viable business. This plan establishes policies for the family's role in the business. For example, it may include an entry and exit policy that outlines the criteria for working in the business. It should include the creed or mission statement that spells out your family's values and basic policies for the business. The family strategic plan will address other issues that are important to your family. By implementing this plan, you may avoid later conflicts about compensation, sibling rivalry, ownership and management control.

- A succession plan will ease the founding or current generation's concerns about transferring the firm. It outlines how succession will occur and how to know when the successor is ready. Many founders do not want to let go of the company because they are afraid the successors are not prepared, or they are afraid to be without a job. Often, heirs sense this reluctance and plan an alternative career. If, however, the heirs see a plan in place that outlines the succession process, they may be more apt to continue in the family business.

- An estate plan is critical for the family and the business. Without it, you will pay higher estate taxes than necessary. Taking the time to develop an estate plan ensures that your estate goes primarily to your heirs rather than to taxes.

For business owners who do little planning, the idea of preparing four plans may seem overwhelming. Although it is not easy, the commitment made by all family members during the planning process is the key ingredient for business continuity and success. The first rule for successfully operating and transferring the family firm is: Share information with all family members, active and nonactive. By doing this, you will eliminate problems that arise when decisions are made and implemented without the knowledge and counsel of all family members.

UNDERSTANDING THE FAMILY BUSINESS

This section will explore the nature of the family business as a dual operating system, and will identify issues of greatest concern to family business owners, as identified by family business owners across the country. As you review these issues, you will see that, although you and your family are unique, the challenges you face are not, because almost every family business shares the same problems.

Also, perspectives of the individuals involved in a family business will be presented. We tend to confuse personality with perspective--understanding the viewpoints of the different actors involved in the family business (active and nonactive) can help alleviate conflicts that may arise.

What Is a Family Business?

Defined simply, a family business is any business in which a majority of the ownership or control lies within a family, and in which two or more family members are directly involved. It is also a complex, dual system consisting of the family and the business; family members involved in the business are part of a task system (the business) and part of a family system. These two systems overlap. This is where conflict may occur because each system has its own rules, roles and requirements. For example, the family system is an emotional one, stressing relationships and rewarding loyalty with love and with care. Entry into this system is by birth, and membership is permanent. The role you have in the family--husband/father, wife/mother, child/brother/sister--carries with it certain responsibilities and expectations. In addition, families have their own style of communicating and resolving conflicts, which they have spent years perfecting. These styles may be good for family situations but may not be the best ways to resolve business conflicts.

Conversely, the business system is unemotional and contractually based. Entry is based on experience, expertise and potential. Membership is contingent upon performance, and performance is rewarded materially. Like the family system, roles in the business, such as president, manager, employee and stockholder/owner, carry specific responsibilities and expectations. And like the home environment, businesses have their own communication, conflict resolution and decision-making styles.

Conflicts arise when roles assumed in one system intrude on roles in the other, when communication patterns used in one system are used in the other or when there are conflicts of interest between the two systems. For example, a conflict may arise between parent and child, between siblings or between a husband and wife when roles assumed in the business system carry over to the family system. The boss and employee roles a husband and wife might assume at work most likely will not be appropriate as at-home roles. Alternatively, a role assumed in the family may not work well in the business. For instance, offspring who are the peace makers at home may find themselves mediating management conflicts between family members whether or not they have the desire or qualifications to do so.

A special case of role carryover may occur when an individual is continually cast in a particular role. This happens primarily to children. Everyone grows up with a label: the good one, the black sheep, the smart one. While a person may outgrow a label, the family often perceives that person as still carrying the attribute. This perception may affect the way that person operates in the business.

Family communication patterns don't always affect the business, but when they do it can be very embarrassing. Often you say things to family members in a way you would never speak to other employees or managers. This problem is compounded when your communication is misread by the family member. Often parents are surprised by a son's or daughter's negative reaction to a business directive or performance evaluation. This reaction is probably because the individual perceived the instructions or evaluation as orders or criticism from Dad or Mom, not from the boss.

System overlap is apparent when conflicts of interest arise between the family and the business.

Some families put personal concerns before business concerns instead of trying to achieve a balance between the two. It is important to understand that the family's strong emotional attachments and overriding sense of loyalty to each other create unique management situations. For example, solving a family problem, such as giving an unemployable or incompetent relative a position in the firm, ignores the company's personnel needs but meets the needs of family loyalty.

Another example of conflict of interest occurs when business owners feel that giving children equal salaries is fair. Siblings who have more responsibility but receive the same pay as those with less responsibility usually resent it. In cases of sibling rivalry, it isn't unusual for one sibling to withhold information from another or try to engage in power plays, i.e., behaviors that can be detrimental to the firm.

Much of this behavior can be eliminated or managed by devising policies that meet the needs of both the family and the business. Developing these policies is part of the family strategic planning process. Before discussing them, you should make sure you have identified all the issues that need to be addressed.

Issues in the Family Businesses

The list below contains the issues that most family businesses face:

Participation--who can participate in the family business and under what circumstances.

Leadership and ownership--how to prepare the next generation to assume responsibility for the business.

Letting go--how to help the entrepreneur let go of the family business.

Liquidity and estate taxes.

Attracting and retaining non-family executives.

Compensation of family members--equality versus merit.

Successors--who chooses and how to choose among multiple successors.

Strengthening family harmony.

All of these issues and the others you include in the Family Business Assessment Inventory can potentially cause business conflict and family stress. But there are three steps you can take to manage conflict and stress in a family business:

Identify issues that may cause conflict and stress. Discuss these issues with the family. Devise a policy to address them.

Who Are the Actors?

The next consideration in understanding the family business is to understand the perspectives of those involved. Without this understanding, managing a family business will be difficult.

The actors in the family business can be divided into two groups: (1) family members and (2) non-family members. Each group has its own perspective and set of concerns and is capable of exerting pressures within the family and the firm.

Family Members

Neither an Employee nor an Owner - Children and in-laws are usually in this group. Although they may not be part of the business operations, they can exert pressure within the family that affects the business. For example, children may resent the time a parent spends in the business. This creates a problem because parents usually develop guilt feelings as a result of their neglect and the resentment expressed by the children. In-laws, on the other hand, are viewed either as outsiders and intruders or as allies and therefore are usually ignored or misunderstood. For example, a daughter-in-law is usually expected to support her husband's efforts in the business without a clear understanding of family or business dynamics. She may contribute to family problems or find herself in the middle of a family struggle. The son-in-law faces similar, if not worse, problems. He may be placed in a competitive situation with his wife's brothers. If he isn't involved in the family business, he can still exert pressure on the business in his role as his wife's confidant.

An Employee but not an Owner - This family member works in the business but does not have an ownership position. For this individual, conflict may arise for a number of reasons.

For example, if he or she compares himself or herself to the family member who has an ownership position but is not an employee, a sense of inequity may result. The member may voice his or her resentment: I'm doing all the work, and they just sit back and get all the profits. Or resentment may occur when decisions are made by owners alone. Here, he or she may feel: I'm working here every day. I know how decisions are going to affect the company. Why didn't they ask me? Family members employed in or associated with a family business generally expect to be treated differently from non-family employees.

An Employee and an Owner - This individual may have the most difficult position. He or she must effectively handle all the actors in both systems. As an owner, he or she is responsible for the well-being and continuance of the business, as well as the daily business operations. He or she must deal with the concerns of both family and non-family employees. Often, the founder, as the sole owner and chief executive, falls in this category.

Not an Employee but an Owner - This group usually consists of siblings and retired relatives. Their major concern usually is the income provided by the business; thus, anything that threatens their security may cause conflict. For example, if the managing owners want to pursue a growth strategy that will consume cash and has an element of risk, they may face resistance from retired relatives who are concerned primarily about dividend payments.

Non-family Members

An Employee but not an Owner - This group deals with the issues of nepotism and coalition building and the effects of family conflicts on daily operations. Owners' concerns for non-owner employees usually involve recruiting and motivating non-family employees and non-family owner-managers who will have little or no opportunity for advancement, accepting children of non-family managers into the business and minimizing political moves that support family members over non-owner employees.

An Employee and an Owner - With the emergence of stock-option plans, this group has become more important. Employees may become owners during a succession. In companies where a successor has been chosen, partial ownership of the company by its employees can foster cooperation with the new management because the employees will personally share the benefits and responsibilities of the company. In cases where there is no successor, selling the company to the employees who have helped build it makes good business sense. Employees who own the company will want to be treated like owners, which may be difficult for family members to understand and accept. A thorough understanding of the behavioral consequences of an employee stock ownership program (ESOP) should be grasped before a family implements such a program. Understanding the perspective of the individuals around you, both family and non-family, will make communicating and decision making easier.

3. How to Balance Family And Business Goals

When conflict occurs in the family run business, it can be traced to a disparity in the goals of the individuals, the family or the business. Perhaps a family member works in the business out of economic necessity, not because he or she wants to. Or perhaps the potential successor has plans for the family run business that differ from current management plans--different generations usually have different goals. Whatever the cause, the conflict must be addressed and resolved to avoid and prevent more serious problems later.

One way to define and align family and business goals is through business and family strategic planning. In these plans, you will create a mission statement for the business and for the family that allows each element to complement the other. Once you have completed this task, set goals for the family business that will allow the family and business to prosper. Next, develop a strategy to accomplish these goals and, finally, formulate policies and procedures that control the family's involvement in the business.

Business Strategic Planning

Strategic planning for family-owned businesses requires that you integrate family issues, such as:

What are the long-term personal and professional

goals of family members?

What is the family mission? Why are you committed to establishing and operating the business?

How do you envision the firm in the future?

Will family members be active in management or will they be passive members?

How will issues such as compensation, benefits and performance evaluation be handled?

The answers to these questions will affect the business strategy and should be resolved before strategic planning begins.

Strategic planning involves analyzing the family run business in its environment and devising a process for guiding its development and success in the future. This process involves assessing the internal operations and the current external environment (i.e., economic, technological, social and political forces) that affect the business. To begin this process, identify internal strengths and weaknesses that may constrain or support a strategy. Components of this assessment include (1) the organizational structure, (2) the culture and (3) the resources. Make a list of the opportunities available (growth, new markets, a change in regulations) and the threats (increased competition, shortage of raw materials, price cutting) to your business. This should give you some insight into the current situation and provide a strategic direction.

Next, list the objectives of you and your family, identifying personal needs and risk orientation. Many of these objectives and goals will be addressed in your family strategic plan. Also, you will find that your personal objectives will affect the strategy you choose. For example, if there is a great opportunity for growth in your market but you have a low risk orientation and a high personal need for security, you probably should not pursue high growth. It would be not only risky but also expensive. Growth consumes cash, and cash must be generated internally or financed externally. Your personal objectives should mesh with your strategy.

Once you have identified opportunities in the industry, assessed the strengths and weaknesses of the firm and listed your personal objectives, you can proceed with the strategic plan. This will involve

developing a mission statement,

setting objectives,

developing strategies to meet objectives, and

developing action steps to implement the strategy.

Mission Statement

The mission statement answers the question "What business are you in?" It defines your customers and explains why you are in business. The mission statement embodies the heart of the business and gives direction to every facet of the business. Effective mission statements

include specifications that allow measurement,

establish the individuality of the firm,

define the business in which the firm wants to be involved,

are relevant to all with a stake in the firm, and

are exciting and inspiring.

Objectives

You should set reasonable objectives for the firm, based on the mission statement, to ensure accomplishment of the firm's mission. Objectives should be clearly stated, realistic, measurable, time specific and challenging. Objectives can be created for:

revenue growth,

earnings growth,

sales and market share growth,

new plants or stores, and

product/service quality or corporate image.

Strategies

Strategies are determined by your answer to the earlier question: "What will the firm be like in the future?" Your strategic options include the following:

Stability--success is derived from little change (rare).

Profit strategy--sacrifice future growth for profits today.

Growth strategy--growth may be achieved through vertical integration (expansion from within), horizontal integration (buy a competitor), diversification, merger or retrenchment (turnaround or divestment).

Action Steps

Once the strategy is selected, action steps should be specified that will guide the firm's daily activities. An example of an action step is creating a budget to project the costs of a strategy. This process also is known as tactical planning. The steps in tactical planning should be practical and easy to implement and account for; their purpose is to convert goals into manageable, realistic steps that can be individually implemented.

Family Strategic Planning

The entire family should develop a mission statement or creed that defines why it is committed to the business. By sharing priorities, strengths and weaknesses, and the contribution each member can make to the business, the family will begin to create a unified vision of the firm. This vision will include personal goals and career objectives.

An important issue to consider is how to set priorities for the family and the business, i.e., decide which will come first, the family or the business. How you answer this question will influence your planning. Some family members will opt for the business first, reasoning that, without a business, there will be no financial security for the family. Others will opt for the family first, reasoning that no business is worth the loss of family harmony. A third alternative is to serve both family and business perhaps not equally, but as fairly as possible. Under this alternative, all decisions are made to satisfy both family and business objectives. For example, a family may have a policy that any family member may join the business, but he or she must meet the requirements of the job. You may find this is the best alternative because it forces a commitment to both the family and the business.

The Family Retreat

Trying to plan a business strategy during normal office hours is almost impossible. Plan a family business retreat to discuss the goals of the individual family members and the goals of the business. The first retreat should focus on reviewing the firm's history, defining family and business values and missions, creating a statement about the future of the business and reviewing areas that need more attention.

The purpose of the retreat is to provide a forum for introspection, problem solving and policy making. For some participants this will be their first opportunity to talk about their concerns in a non-confrontational atmosphere. It is also a time to celebrate the family and enhance its inner strength.

A retreat usually lasts two days and is held far enough away so you won't be disturbed or tempted to go to the office. Every member of the family, including in-laws, should be invited. Begin planning your retreat about six weeks in advance.

Once you have picked a time and place, establish a tentative agenda. Your actual agenda will be tailored to meet the unique needs of your family and business. Usually families will identify some of the following issues for discussion at their first retreat:

A family creed or mission statement.

Management succession.

Estate planning.

Strategic business planning.

The reward system.

Performance evaluation.

Communication within the family.

Preparing adult children to enter the business.

Transition timing.

Exit and entry policies.

You may consider using a retreat facilitator, a professional experienced in helping family-owned businesses. The facilitator helps identify issues for discussion before the retreat and keeps the atmosphere non-confrontational during the retreat. The facilitator does not solve the family's problems but guides the family in doing so.

The retreat is the beginning of a process. When a consensus is reached by the participants, policies should be set, courses of action planned and responsibility for implementation assigned. When agreement cannot be reached, further discussions should be planned, possibly with the continued assistance of the facilitator.

One important outcome of the retreat should be plans for periodic family meetings and retreats in the future, so the dialogue will continue. Open communications will enable the family to come to grips with problems and issues while they are fairly easy to solve. Once family members have reached a consensus on the continuity of the firm and their roles in it, you can begin planning for succession.

4. Common Problems and How to Solve Them

Management problems in a family business owned are somewhat different from the same problems in a non-family business. When close relatives work together, emotions often interfere with business decisions.

In some family companies, control of daily operations is a problem. In others, a high turnover rate among non-family members is a problem. In still other companies, growth is a problem because some of the relatives are unwilling to plow profits back into the business.

This family business owned guide discusses such problems from the viewpoint of the family member who is the company's manager. It offers suggestions that should help you to manage effectively and profitably.

When you put up your own money and operate your own business. you prize your independence. "It's my business," you tell yourself in good times and in bad times.

However, "it's our business," in a family company. Conflicts sometimes abound because relatives look upon the business from different viewpoints.

Those relatives who are silent partners, stockholders, and directors see only dollar signs when judging capital expenditures, growth, and other major matters. Relatives who are engaged in daily operations judge major matters from the viewpoint of the production, sales, and personnel necessary to make the company successfully. Obviously, these two viewpoints may conflict in many instances.

This natural conflict can be aggravated by family members who have no talent for money or business. Sometimes they are the weak offspring of the founders of the company-sons and daughters who lack business acumen-and sometimes they are in-laws who must be taken care of regardless of their ability or the company's needs.

Basically, the management problems that face the manager of a family-owned business are the same as those which confront the owner-manager of any small company. But the job of the "family manager" is complicated because of the relatives who must be reconciled to the facts of the market place, the factory, and the counting house.

The Sparks Fly

Different opinions do not always produce discord, but sometimes they cause "sparks to fly" - especially in a family-owned company. Emotion is an added dimension as brothers and sisters, uncles and aunts, nephews and nieces and fathers and children work together in such a small business.

For the individual who must head such a company, the important thing is to recognize this dimension of emotions and to make objective decisions that are difficult to come by in such situations.

Many times when members of a family are active in the business, it is hard to make objective decisions about the skills and abilities of each other. For example, one says about another relative, "He was lazy when we were kids, and he's still lazy." Or a disgruntled wife says about an aunt. "What does she know about the business? She's only here because of her father's money."

If such emotional outbursts affected only the family, the manager might "knock a few heads together" and move along. But often it is not that easy. The quarrels and ill feelings of relatives have a way of spreading out to include non-family employees.

Then the manager's problem is to keep the bickering from interfering with work. You cannot afford to let the company become divided into warring camps. You have to convince non-family employees that their interests are best served by a profitable organization rather than by allegiance to particular members of the family.

Another aspect of the emotional atmosphere is that often non-family employees tend to base their decisions on the family's tensions. They know how their bosses react and are influenced by this knowledge.

Is The Manager Really In Control?

The president of a small company is not always necessarily the person in charge. In many family-owned businesses, the elder statesman of the family becomes president or chairman of the board of directors. But day-to-day management is in the hands of other members of the family.

In some cases, even the best hands are tied as the family member tries to manage the business. For example, the ceiling on the amount of money that can be spent without permission from the rest of the family may be too low for the situation confronting the company. Having to clear operating expenditures may mean missing opportunities for increased profits, such as taking advantage of a good price on raw materials or sales inventory.

In other cases, a manager may be in a bind because of emotional involvement. For example, you may feel that you have to clear routine matters with top family members because "Uncle Bill never lets you forget your mistakes." Personalities and emotional reactions create bottlenecks that work against an efficient operation.

Efficiency may be reduced also by relatives who indulge in excessive family talk during working hours. The manager should set the example and insist that relatives refrain from family chit-chat on the job.

In some family-owned companies, the day-to-day manager may be a bottleneck. You may be a bottleneck because you do not have the ability to delegate work and authority. You may be the manager because of age or the amount of capital you have in the business without regard to your qualifications. In other instances, you may hold up progress because you do not listen to others in the company.

One solution is for other members of the family to persuade such a manager to let someone else run the day-to-day show, perhaps a hired manager.

If a member of the family has to be in charge of operations, he or she should be capable of using efficient management techniques and be thick-skinned enough to live with family bickering and tough enough to make his or her decisions stick.

One way to obtain objective control in a family-owned business is to hire an outsider to manage the day-to-day operations, when the company can afford it. Any manager may become as biased as any other family member. With a hired manager, the family members will have their hands full in setting policies and in planning for growth. An efficient hired manager will see to it that all employees - family and non-family alike - know to whom to report at all times.

Such definite lines of authority are even more important when a member of the family manages operations with other relatives filling various jobs. The responsibilities of family members should be spelled out. "Family employees" should discipline themselves to work within the bounds of these lines of authority. Even then, it is wise to have a non-family employee high in the organization so that he or she can be involved in operations and help smooth out any emotional decisions which family members may make.

The manager's authority to suspend or discharge flagrant violators of company rules should also be spelled out. Management control is weakened if special allowances are made for "family employees".

An important question connected with authority is: Who takes over when something happens to the family member who heads the business? A position may be "up for grabs" if the family hasn't provided for an orderly succession. This need is especially critical when the top family member is approaching retirement age or is in poor health.

Your Brother-In-Law Needs A Job?

One of the most common problems in a family business is the hiring of relatives who do not have talent. But what are you to do when your sister or another close relative says, "Bob needs a job badly"? The emotional aspect of such family relationships is hard to fight. But try to go into it with your eyes open. It will be hard to fire Bob if he turns out to cost you more money than his presence is worth.

The main thing is to recognize the talent or lack of it. Suppose your brother-in-law, for example, has little or no ability as far as your company is concerned, Perhaps you can put him in a job where in spite of his weaknesses he can make a contribution and not disturb other employees.

The major concern is not necessarily the relative but how he or she affects other employees. In some cases, a relative can demoralize the organization by his or her dealing with other employees. For example, he or she may loaf on the job, avoid unpleasant tasks, take special privileges, and make snide remarks about you and other relatives.

If you are stuck with such a relative, try putting him or her in a job where he or she will have minimum contact with other employees, out of the mainstream of decision making. For instance brother-in-law Bob might be placed in a sales office in another city some distance from the company's headquarters where he will be under the supervision of a top producer. Another alternative is to change his attitudes by formal or informal education.

The key is to see that the non-talented relative does not affect the relationship that you, the manager, have with other members of your staff. Other employees will respect you for keeping relatives in line.

Strange things sometimes happen. There is always the chance that the non-talented relative may be under your direction and turn into an asset for your company.

Is Non-family Turnover High?

Some family-owned companies are plagued with a high turnover among their non-family top people. Sometimes relatives are responsible. They resent outside talent and, at best, make things unpleasant for non-family executives.

In other cases, top notch managers and workers leave because promotions are closed to them.

They see your relatives being pushed into executive offices.

The exit interview is a useful device for getting at the root of this type of turnover. A key employee who has decided to leave may be eager to tell you the true story - or at least enough of the facts to help you develop a course of action.

When a manager has the facts, he or she may have to confront the trouble-causing relative with an unpleasant story. What comes out of the confrontation is anyone's guess. Rare is the owner-manager who can fire a troublesome and close relative and make it stick. One way to remove such a thorn from the side of key executives is to help the relative start a business in a noncompeting line-provided he or she has the management ability that is necessary for success. Another way is to "exile" him or her to a branch office or find a job with another company.

Spending To Save Money?

Many times, as the owner-manager you feel that you must make an expenditure to improve efficiency, yet other family members oppose the expenditure. They view it as an expense rather than an investment. They feel that funds spent for items, such as more efficient equipment, encroach in their year-end dividends.

One way to help these relatives see that "you have to spend money to make money" is to base your arguments for the expenditures on facts and figures that non-family employees have gathered. Suggest to the opposing family members that the matter be settled on a cold dollar basis: for example, "by spending money for this machine, we can increase profits and get our money back in four years."

If the opposing relatives refuse to accept your projection, try calling in outside business advisers. Relatives will sometimes believe advisers, such as your banker, accountant, or attorney, when they won't accept your judgment. But keep in mind that outside advisers who are personally close to other family members, should not be included among your counselors.

Paid consultants can also be useful in proving the worth of an expenditure. Such help is particularly valuable on specialized projects that require more research that you or your regular advisers have time to do.

Status Quo Blocks Growth

When some of the relatives in a family-owned business grow older, they develop an attitude of status quo. They don't want things to change and are afraid of risk. With this attitude, they can, and often do, block growth in their family's business.

The solution to such a problem is to urge or suggest that the status quo members slowly disappear from the scene of operation. One way to do this is to dilute their influence in management decisions. For example, the status quo relatives might be given the opportunity to convert their stock in the corporation to preferred stock. Or they might sell some of their stock to the younger relatives.

It might also be possible for the status quo relatives to think in terms of gradual retirement. Their salaries can be reduced over several years, and they can relinquish some of their interests. With the proper legal advice, it might be possible for a small corporation to re-capitalize. A new partnership agreement might be drawn up when the company is a partnership.

Such actions can take into account all of the growth of the business to that particular point and can enable the retreating members to recover their equity. Meanwhile, the manager and active relatives can renew their efforts toward expanding the business.

How Is The Pie Divided?

Paying family, members and dividing profits among them can also be a difficult affair. Many persons feel that they are underpaid, but what about relatives who comment as follows:

"Uncle Jack sits around and gets more than I do."

"Aunt Sue goes to Europe on the returns of money her husband put into the business before he died ten years ago."

"Your brother goofs off and rakes in more than you do."

How do you resolve such complaints? You don't entirely. But if the business is a small corporation, certain equalizing factors can be accomplished by stock dividends. By re-capitalizing the company, some stockholders can take preferred stock with dividends.

Salaries are best handled by being competitive with those paid in the area. Find out what local salary ranges are for various management jobs and use these ranges as a guide for paying both family and non-family personnel. When you tie pay to the type of work that the individual does, you can show disgruntled relatives the value that the industry puts on their jobs.

Fringe benefits can also be useful in dividing profits equitably among family members. Benefits, such as deferred profit sharing plans, pension plans, insurance programs, and stock purchase programs, offer excellent ways to placate disgruntled members of the family and at the same time help them to build their personal assets.

How the pie is divided is vital to growth in a small business. Profits are the seedbed for expansion, and lenders are influenced by what is done with profits. What banker wants to lend a company a substantial amount when its earned surplus is drained off by relatives?

Where Do You Go For Money?

Another major problem in managing a family business is that of obtaining money for growth. Generally speaking if the company is profitable, you can get funds from your bank.

But when the growth is substantial, a company often outgrows its local bank. When you see the prospect of expansion looming ahead, the managing relative should begin to plan for it. You will need to consider techniques for financing, such as the following. Planned financing may be a combination of these items:

Taking out a mortgage on the company's building.

Asking suppliers to extend credit on purchases.

Factoring the company's receivables and inventory financing.

Borrowing on a note basis from friends.

Borrowing the cash surrender value of relatives' life insurance policies.

Contacting an insurance company for a long-term loan.

If the business is a small corporation, the following techniques also offer possible sources of money:

Selling a portion of the stock to the company's employees for cash.

Selling some of the stock to another company for cash. In a merger, you can use the credit of the larger company.

Contacting a regional investment banker who may privately find a lender, using some of the company's stock as collateral.

Contacting a national investment banker who would underwrite some of the company's stock. This would be "going public".

Effective budgetary controls are important in seeking growth funds. Such controls help the managing relative to determine the company's needs. Lenders also regard them as evidence of good management.

Exchange Information

Fortunately, in most communities, the manager of a family-owned business is not alone. Other individuals operate small companies for their families and may provide a source of information and help.

The managing relative should seek out and cultivate counterparts. You can exchange ideas with them and learn how they solved problems in which their relatives were involved.

In a small corporation, the thinking can be stimulated by having outsiders on the board of directors - directors who are not relatives and who are from other types of businesses.

Trade associations are also good sources of information and help. Through them, the managing relative can get facts from non-competitors.

5. How to Choose a Successor

Succession is the transferring of leadership to the next generation. It is a process rather than an event. While there is a time frame within which the transition will occur, the actual amount of time taken for the process is arbitrary. It will depend on you, your family and the type of family business you are in. This is a difficult process for most family businesses. The failure to face and plan for succession has been termed the "succession conspiracy" by Ivan Landsberg. He cites a number of forces that act against succession planning:

Founder

Fear of death.

Reluctance to let go of power and control.

Personal loss of identity.

Fear of losing work activity.

Feelings of jealousy and rivalry toward successor.

Family

Founder's spouse's reluctance to let go of role in firm.

Norms against discussing family's future beyond lifetime of parents.

Norms against "favoring" siblings.

Fear of parental death.

Employees

Reluctance to let go of personal relationship with founder.

Fears of differentiating among key managers.

Reluctance to establish formal controls.

Fear of change

Environmental

Founder's colleagues and friends continue to work.

Dependence of clients on founder.

Cultural values that discourage succession planning.

Overcoming the forces against succession planning requires the commitment of the family and employees of the business.

Succession occurs in four phases: initiation, selection, education and transition. A discussion of each phase follows.

Initiation

The initiation phase is that period of time when the children learn about the family business. It occurs from the time the children are born. A child can receive either a positive or a negative impression of the family business. If parents bring home the negative aspects of the business, complaining about it and about employees and relatives, the children will view the business in a very poor light. Other ways to destroy children's interest in the business is to be secretive about it or to convey an unwelcome or a hands-off attitude. There are families in which children are welcome to join the family business, but no one has told them so.

Owners are often cautious about systematically conditioning their children to enter the family business, an attitude that stems primarily from their awareness of individual differences and their belief that their children should be free to select a career path. If you do want your children to enter the business, or at least have that as a career alternative, there are some steps you can take to initiate them into the firm. The first step in motivating your children is to be certain that is what you want. Your lack of conviction about their involvement will be communicated to them. This may be interpreted as doubt about their ability, about the viability of the business or about the potential of the parent-child relationship to survive the strain of succession. Any of these situations can cause your child to lose interest in the business.

Assuming your children know that you want them to enter the business, you should talk with them often and openly about it. Be realistic, but stress the positive aspects. Your business provides you with many positive experiences to share with your children. Your children should learn what values the business represents, what the business culture represents and where the business is headed.

Selection

Selection is the process of choosing who will be the firm's leader in the next generation. Of the entire transition process, this can be the most difficult step, especially if you must choose among a number of children. Selecting a successor may be viewed by siblings as favoring one child over the others, a perception that can be disastrous to family well-being and sibling harmony. Owners select successors on the basis of age, sex, qualifications or performance. Because of the potential for emotional upheaval, some owners avoid the issue entirely, adopting an attitude of "Let them figure it out when I'm gone."

Nevertheless, there are several solutions to this dilemma. Assuming you have more than one child who is or can become qualified for the position of president, you can select your successor based on age. For example, the oldest child becomes the successor. Unfortunately, the oldest may not be the best qualified. Placing age or sex restrictions on succession is not a good idea.

Alternatively, you could have a "horse race." Let the candidates fight it out, and the "best person" wins. While this is the style in some major corporations, it is not the best option for all family businesses.

Family business owners may want to take advantage of a successor selection model developed for corporate executive succession. In this model, family members, using the strategic business plan, develop specific company objectives and goals for the future president or chief executive officer. The job description includes the requirements for the position--such as skills, experience and possibly personality attributes. For example, if a firm plans to pursue growth in the next five years, the potential successor would be required to have a thorough understanding of business valuations and financial statements, the ability to negotiate and a good relationship with local financial institutions.

Designing such job descriptions provides a number of benefits. First, it removes the emotional aspect from successor selection. If necessary, the successor can acquire any special training the job description outlines. Second, it provides the business with a set of future goals and objectives that have been developed by the whole family. Finally, the founder may feel more comfortable knowing objectives are in place that will ensure a growing, healthy business.

If you have an outside board of directors, you may want to solicit their input regarding successor selection.

Education

Training or educating the successor in the firm is a delicate process. Many times a parent finds it difficult to train a child to be successor. If so, an alternative trainer may be found within the firm. A successful trainer will be logical, committed to the task, credible and action oriented. These attributes, when tied into a program that is mission aligned, results oriented, reality-driven, learner centered and risk sensitive, will produce a well-trained beneficiary. All of this, of course, is easier stated than accomplished.

A training variant of the management by objectives (MBO) concept is the training by objectives (TBO) concept. This concept can be an effective method for providing both the training for and the evaluation of successors. In the TBO process, both the trainer (you or a non-family manager) and the trainee (potential successor) work together to define what the trainee will do, the time period for action and the evaluation process to be used. This system allows the successor to be placed in a useful, responsible position with well-delineated objectives. It also provides for steps of increased responsibility as goals are met and new, more rigorous goals are established. It is important that the successor enter the firm in a well-defined position. Instead of entering the company as "assistant to the president," which requires that he or she follow the president around all day, the successor (or any other child) should enter with a specific job description. In a small business this is very difficult because everyone is usually responsible for all tasks. Nevertheless, the successor cannot be evaluated effectively if he or she is not given responsibility and authority for certain tasks.

Your business will enable you to determine which criteria are necessary for good training. Usually, an owner wants to assess a successor in the following areas:

Decision-making process.

Leadership abilities.

Risk orientation.

Interpersonal skills.

Temperament under stress.

An excellent way to assess these skills is to let the successor give his or her insight on a current problem or situation. This is not a test and should not be confrontational. Instead, solicit advice and try to determine the thinking process that is generating your successor's suggestions. For example, you may be faced with a pricing decision. Give the successor all the information needed to determine whether or not to raise prices, then sit back and listen. Ask questions when appropriate-- these should be "Why?" and "What if?" After the successor is finished, say "I was considering. . . ." This way each of you can learn how the other thinks and makes decisions.

It is possible that your leadership style differs from that of your successor. Your employees are used to your style. If your successor's style is very autocratic and uncaring, your company is going to experience problems.

Potential successors should be introduced into your outside network (e.g., customers, bankers and business associates), something many managers neglect. This will give everyone time to get to know your successor and allow the successor to work with business associates and bankers, and to get acquainted with customers.

Transition

The actual transfer of control to the successor occurs when you retire. Research indicates that transitions are smoothest when

They are timely.

They are final and do not include the entrepreneur's participation in daily activities.

The entrepreneur is publicly committed to an orderly succession plan.

The entrepreneur has articulated and supervised the formulation of company principles regarding management accountability, policies, objectives and strategies.

The transition can be effected gradually by relinquishing more and more responsibility to the successor. One expert advises the entrepreneur to take a number of planned absences before actually relinquishing control. Let the successor see what it is like to manage the business alone. Also, this allows you to see that the business is not going to fall apart without you.

Once you announce your retirement date, do not rescind it. There is no such thing as semi-retirement. By the time your children are in their 40s, they expect leadership roles in the firm. If you refuse to let go, they may leave.

Letting Go

There are many reasons why entrepreneurs cannot let go of the family business. Primary among these are financial ones. As a business owner, you may be used to a large salary and benefits, such as a car or insurance. After working hard in the business most of your life, you want your retirement years to be comfortable, not filled with financial anxieties. There are several ways to ensure your financial security after retirement. Business owners usually consider either taking what they need from the company after they retire or arranging a buy-out that will give them the needed liquidity without placing an undue financial burden on the company. If you don't sell the company and your financial security is contingent on its daily operations, you will be less likely to retire completely. Your successor needs full control, and you probably won't let that happen. Also, the company may not be able to support you and the successor and still pursue the strategy you have set for it. Finally, you may not be able to meet your financial goals from income generated by the company.

To avoid these problems, consult with a financial planner or an attorney to determine the method of transfer that is best for you. There are tax consequences to the outright sale of the business to your children. Also, an outright sale may burden the company with too much debt. Other alternatives include an installment sale or private annuity, or funding a buy-sell with insurance proceeds. To provide effectively for your retirement, seek professional assistance in this area.

There are other reasons why the entrepreneur doesn't want to let go. One of the primary reasons is the fear of retirement. To understand this fear, it is necessary to appreciate the relationship between work, the meaning of life and social evaluation. For many founders, work and the business are synonymous with a meaningful life. The intense involvement the entrepreneur has with the business increases the importance of the job and his or her identity. Removal from work is like losing a part of oneself. Work is important to the entrepreneur because it provides:

Economic returns.

Opportunities to contribute to society.

Status and self-respect.

Social interaction.

Personal identity.

Structured time.

Escape from loneliness and isolation.

Personal achievement.

That's a lot to ask someone to give up. Especially important is the loss of status and social power. The leader of a firm wields a great deal of influence and enjoys public impact and public exposure. Retirement means giving up this power. Because this loss is unpleasant, it is not uncommon for a founder to give a successor the responsibility for running a firm and still try to retain power and privileges from a position on the board of directors.

The entrepreneur who successfully lets go has:

(1) a sound financial plan for retirement,

(2) activities outside the business that can provide social contact and power,

(3) confidence in the successor and

(4) a willingness to listen to outside advisors.

Board of Directors

Most small businesses do not have a board of directors, but a board can be invaluable during the succession process. A board can help management determine objectives and strategies, provide specialized expertise and even arbitrate feuds among family members.

The board is usually composed of both insiders and outsiders. Although family businesses usually are operated in a very private manner, there are benefits to making outsiders board members. They come with different backgrounds and perspectives, and provide checks and balances. Outside directors don't work out well if they lack knowledge about the firm and its environment, or if they are uncommitted to board responsibilities.

If you decide to develop a board, you should be totally committed to the process. There are difficulties associated with boards (time and money) and the entrepreneur must be willing to make the board a viable entity.

The first step would be to establish goals and objectives for the board. You should set these objectives before you recruit or make a commitment to any members. Boards can expand your network, provide input into the succession process, judge the successor's progress or help determine a transition date. But boards should not get overly involved in operational or day-to-day issues.

The second step is recruiting. A board should have five to seven members, including three or four outsiders. Select them carefully. You can find them in civic and charitable organizations, among acquaintances and at local universities. You should know and have a good rapport with prospective members, and you should determine their ability to provide concrete advice and direction for the business. The following are a few good questions to ask:

What is their background?

How are they thought of in the community?

What do your present directors think of them?

Make sure they have the qualifications to help realize the goals and objectives you have set. The remainder of the board is composed of top insiders. Your potential successor may be invited to attend the meetings, or you may choose to make him or her a member of the board.

Making Succession Work

To make succession work, you must communicate. This is the key ingredient. Use the family retreat as well as family meetings. Family meetings can educate the family in discussions about the nature of the firm, the kinds of leadership skills needed, entry and exit conditions, decision-making policies and conflict resolution procedures. Casual conversations about these issues can contribute to your formal planning later on.

Family meetings do not have to be formal affairs, but they should occur regularly and have an agenda. Parents don't have to lead the meeting; have the offspring organize and conduct a portion of the meeting. Use the meetings to defuse any potential time bombs.

Anticipate problems. Will there be any problems with non-family members? If so, which ones? How will they be a problem, and what can you do (short of firing them) to handle it?

Sibling rivalry is another problem to consider. Does it exist? If so, how will you resolve it?

It may not be a problem until the successor is named. Develop a code of conduct for sibling relations. This code will outline how siblings must act toward each other (i.e., in a way conducive to a healthy business), including how to work together, how to play together and how to keep spouses informed about what's going on. Anticipate problems that may arise and meet them head on.

Summary

Succession is a process that may extend from three to six years or longer depending on your age and on your successor's age. It occurs in phases. Over a period of time, you initiate or educate your children to the family business. After determining a successor, you develop a plan to transfer leadership in the family business. The decision to announce who the successor is and when the transition will occur depends on the family.

There are benefits to making an early announcement, including (1) reassuring employees, suppliers and customers, (2) allowing siblings time to adjust to the decision and to make alternative career decisions, if necessary, and (3) enabling the entrepreneur to plan for retirement.

The fundamental goal should be to pass the family business successfully to the next generation. To do this you must feel financially secure, secure with the company's future goals and plans and secure with your successor.

6. Family Run Business Assessment

Business issues

Yes/No

1. Have goals for sales and profits been set?

2. Do we have a business plan?

3. Do we have a strategic plan?

4. Is the business in good financial standing?

5. Do we have a compensation system?

6. Do we have a performance appraisal system?

7. Do we have a board of directors?

8. Can we attract and retain non family managers?

9. Is the business in a highly competitive industry?

10. Are we experiencing an increase in sales?

Family business issues

1. Do family members know they are welcome to join the firm?

2. Do we have policies for entry into and exit from the firm?

3. Is a system in place to train and develop the successor?

4. Do we have a succession plan?

5. Can family members in the firm effectively communicate?

6. Do we have a system to resolve conflict among family members?

7. Are women welcomed in the business?

8. Is there a minimum amount of sibling rivalry in the firm?

9. Is there a system in place for choosing a successor?

10. Does the family agree on goals for the business?

If you answered no to any item action should be outlined and implemented to address and set policies for that item.

Section II

The following items need to be discussed in the family business:

Leadership succession.

Ownership transfer.

Communication policies.

Compensation policies.

Rights and responsibilities of non-family employees.

Rights and responsibilities of in-laws.

Creating change.

Development of a management team.

Long-term planning for the business.

Obtaining financing.

Financial equity among children.

Resolving conflict.

Hiring and firing practices.

Sibling rivalry.

Organizational relationships.

Working with advisers.

This list should be distributed to every family member. Responses should be compared and issues of concern to family members identified. Unresolved issues should be discussed and polices established to resolve them.

7. Family Business Strategic Plan

Yes/No

1. Have I listed the emerging opportunities in my industry?

2. Have I listed the environmental threats to my firm?

3. Have I listed the internal strengths of my firm?

4. Have I listed the internal weaknesses of my firm?

5. Have my family and I listed our personal goals and objectives?

6. Do I have a mission statement?

7. Have I listed goals (objectives) for the firm?

8. Are the objectives for my firm in line with my family's

personal goals?

9. Are the objectives for my firm in line with the analysis of my

firm's strengths and weaknesses?

10. Have I written a strategy to meet my objectives?

11. Are my actions

- manageable (one year or less)?

- accountable (someone is responsible)?

- reasonable?

8. How to Improve Your Leadership Skills

As a manager in a family owned business part of your success depends on your leadership skills. This chapter, though not directly related to family owned business, feature a list of leadership tips that if adopted can make your job as a manager much easier. To be able to mutually achieve our goals we must be able to relate to others effectively. These effective leadership skills suggestions will help you do just that.

-- Catch people doing things right and then let them know that they are doing things right.

-- Use feedback to stay informed about what other people are doing in your area of responsibility and authority.

-- Have regular, focused meetings regarding the projects that you are responsible for.

-- Provide adequate instructions. Time is lost if things are not done correctly.

-- Train others to do jobs. You cannot do them all, nor can others do them if they have not been trained.

-- Expect others to succeed. It becomes a self-fulfilling prophecy when you believe others are loyal, dedicated and doing a good job.

-- Help others see how they will benefit from doing a job. This is when they truly become motivated.

-- Do not avoid talking to a poor performer. It hurts them, the organization and yourself if the situation is not dealt with.

-- Do not over control others. It is frustrating for them and time consuming for you.

-- Focus on results, not on activities or personalities.

-- Reward people for the results that they produce.

-- Manage by walking around. See what people are doing and listen to what they have to say.

-- Make quality an obsession, especially on smaller items.

Send thank you notes and memos.

-- Provide workers with open, direct, and immediate feedback on their actual performance as compared to expected performance and they tend to correct their own deficiencies.

-- Practice naive listening. Don't talk, just let people explain why they are doing the types of things that they are doing. You will learn many things.

Manage by exception. When things are going well, leave them alone. When a problem occurs, then help.

-- Never seek to place blame. Always focus on the problem.

-- Never ignore a concern of one of your people. While it may seem trivial to you, to the other person it is a problem that will continue to destroy their train of thought.

-- Make it a personal rule and a challenge to respond to someone within 24 hours of hearing their request.

-- Keep memos on bulletin boards to a minimum. People will spend less time standing there reading.

-- Give employees an opportunity to speak their opinions and suggestions without fear of ridicule or reprisal.

-- When you are going to make a change that affects others, get them involved before making the actual change. This increases commitment to make the change work after it is implemented.

-- Put key ideas on small posters to hang around the office.

-- When the environment and your sincerity permit, give the person a hug or a touch.

-- Employees are the only organization resource that can, with training, appreciate in value. All other resources depreciate.

-- People want to be involved in something important. Give them a whole project or a significant piece of the project to work on.

-- Have salary tied into performance appraisal and accomplishing of objectives.

-- Consider sharing distasteful tasks to reduce resentment and hard feelings.

-- Ask, "Will you please do this for me" instead of telling someone just to do it.

-- Eliminate private secretaries in favor of shared secretaries in order to make it easier to even out the work load.

-- If you give employees a basic employee handbook, you will not be interrupted with their questions.

-- Pay attention to small details, the big ones are obvious and get taken care of.

-- Stay open in your thinking. Be open to all new ideas. Do this and you will not be setting up barriers that do not exist.

-- Avoid asking others to do trivial personal items for you.

-- Say thank you to those with whom you associate.

-- A warm smile and strong handshake break barriers.

-- Smile. It helps you feel better and is contagious. The whole organization shudders when the boss is frowning. Likewise it smiles when the boss does.

-- Keep things "light" and have fun rather than being too serious. Seriousness blocks productivity.

-- In order to fly with the eagles you must "think lightly."

-- Work with each person to create standard operating procedures for their specific job. It will eliminate repetitious questions.

-- Let people know why they are doing something. It then becomes more meaningful when they recognize their part in a greater vision.

-- Provide soft, lively background music not slow and not rock.

-- To get a disorganized coffee drinking crew started off more efficiently, begin each day with a 5 to 10 minute meeting just at starting time. They will be focused, set in the right direction and can get right to work.

-- Practice the golden rule in business: Do unto others the way you would have them do unto you. Fairness will then be in your business.

-- Practice the platinum rule in interpersonal relationships. It is "Do unto others, the way they want to be done unto." They will be more apt to stay comfortable when interacting with us when we are able to do things their preferred way.

-- Get others to commit to deadlines by asking, "When can you have that for me?"

-- Nail down commitment by asking, "Do I have your word that you will have that for me then?"

-- Set the stage for cooperation from others by:1) Introducing the idea; 2) Continual stimulation by talking about it; and 3) get others to make an investment by having them participate in the planning.

-- If you are unable to reach agreement or get a commitment from another person in a meeting, agree to disagree, but summarize your understanding in a confirming memo.

-- Giving people recognition generates energy within them. They will then direct that energy toward increased productivity.

-- Tap the potential of those working for you by giving them opportunities to think things through for themselves instead of just telling them how to do something.

-- Always give people the benefit of the doubt. They may not be the cause of a problem. The cause may be beyond their control.

-- Admit it when you do not know the answer to a question posed by a staff member. Then challenge the staff person to research and decide what the best answer is. It will help this person grow.

-- Be persistent and follow up.

-- When you were away and some of your people did an exceptional job, call them at home in the evening when you find out and personally thank them for what they did instead of waiting until the next time you see them.

-- If you know that a person will respond angrily to a particular comment, avoid bringing it up. It is nonproductive and bad for the relationship. In other words, "never kick a skunk."

-- When you appreciate what someone has done, let them know and put it in writing. This can then be added to their personnel file.

-- Have an opinion survey done to determine how people view the organization. That way you can catch any problems while they are still small.

-- Encourage periods of uninterrupted activity such as a daily quiet hour in your department or work group.

-- When asking someone to do something, let

them know what is in it for them and the organization. Do not focus just on what is in it for the organization and yourself.

-- The boss is the strongest model the employees have. Be a positive model as people are watching to see how you behave. They will reflect this in their own behavior. Lead by example.

-- Be a member of the 4 F club with others. Be seen as Fair, Firm, Friendly and having Foresight.

-- Do not help others unless they need and ask for help.

-- Encourage your people to come up with new ideas and ways to do things. Give them credit and recognition for the idea.

-- If a new idea won't work, at least praise the effort of the person so they will come up with future ideas.

-- Once a month meet with each staff member to catch any problems or concerns the person may have as soon as possible before they become a crisis.

-- Be the kind of a person that others want to help

out and work for.

-- Be flexible and do whatever it takes to get the job done. Remember it is results that count, not activities.

-- Generally speaking, getting something done perfectly is usually not as important as getting it done. Perfection has a high cost and it may not be worth it.

-- When giving or receiving information, don't hurry. Take the time needed to truly understand. It prevents future problems and misunderstandings.

-- Whenever you are having an important discussion with a person, before parting, set a specific follow-up date and time and write it in your calendar.

-- Never criticize an employee in front of others. Have all discussions of a corrective nature in private.

-- Hire people with specific skills and interests that match what the organization needs to have accomplished. The better the match, the better the productivity and the more motivated the person.

-- Treat people as people-not things.

-- Flaring in anger will drive others away. If not physically at least mentally,

-- Keep a "warm fuzzy" file for each person a place to keep track of the things you have already complimented them for, and want to compliment them for.

-- Have regular performance review and goal setting sessions with each of your employees at least every three months.

-- Have regular "development discussions" with each of your people in which you discuss only how the individual may grow personally and how you and the organization may be able to support them in doing this.

-- Low morale in workers may be an indication of the boss only talking about negative things or what's wrong. Be sure to balance negative comments with more frequent positive comments.

-- Let your people know you are there to help them not to harass them.

-- Telling people what you plan to do, and when,

can be a catalyst for getting objections and input which you might not otherwise receive.

-- Form an action team to address people's problems right away rather than letting things drag out and perhaps get worse.

-- Instead of saying to another, "What can I do for you?" ask them "What can you do for me on this project?"

-- Do not hold back from discussing the need to improve performance with one of your people.

-- Encourage others to develop their plan of action and give you a detailed explanation.

-- Encourage individuals to compete against themselves to achieve more. Let it be a personal challenge to become better as an individual-not competing with others but self.

-- Check the ratio of positive comments to negative comments that you make to your people. Purposely make more positive comments.

-- Demand accountability.

-- Do things for others. They will be more willing to do things for you.

-- Consider using time off as a reward for getting things done ahead of time.

-- Set up an orientation training program for all new employees. It will help them learn their way around as well as teach them where things are kept and why.

-- Stay informed of subordinates' needs and interests. Projects can be more effectively designed and rotated when you are well informed.

-- If individuals needs some encouragement in taking action, ask them, "What if..." questions to help them see what choices of action are available.

-- Let people know that you know they can do it.

-- Ask questions creatively so the action to be taken is suggested by the person who is to take it.

-- Set up incentives that reward desired performance.

-- Ask others for their estimate of how long it will take to do a project. When possible, agree and hold them accountable for that goal.

-- Take on someone else's routine so they can do what you need done without interruption.

-- Just as with family members, break large chores up into small, fun activities and enjoy doing them with team members.

-- Before an employee leaves on vacation agree on a "must do" list of activities to be completed.

-- Do not be quick to judge others. Learn to listen carefully before coming to conclusions.

-- Consider sharing ideas and responsibility with others rather than just getting someone to do it for you or just doing it yourself.

-- Inspire others to new levels of achievement by using positive encouraging feedback and ideas.

-- Don't just ask someone who is busy to get things done for you; look for the busy person who is getting results. This is a doer, not simply a busy wheel spinner.

-- Believe in the good of people.

-- Do not be a "baby sitter" of others, constantly taking care of them and telling them what to do. Challenge them and help them learn to think and do things for themselves.

-- Consider an incentive plan to reward

productivity gains.

-- Don't do what you can get someone else to do by simply asking.

-- Clearly communicate who you want to do what, by when and at what cost. Then identify who needs to know about it and when they are to be informed.

-- For people you relate to regularly, keep a list of things you need to talk to the person about. Then when you meet with or call them, you can review all the items that have accumulated on your list.

-- Recognize you are not the only one who can do a job right. Trust others to do things for you.

-- Organize, deputize, supervise.

-- Meditate for one minute before starting a new subject or project.

-- Don't worry about who gets the credit for completing a project. Focus on the task To be accomplished and do it.

-- When credit is given to you for completion of a project, be sure to give it to all who were involved. This will nurture the relationships and provide motivation to support you in the future.

-- Be sincerely interested in the people working for and with you.

-- Help others recognize their own importance.

-- Keep a list of birthdays, marriage and work anniversaries and other special dates. Provide recognition to your people on each of these dates. Mark your calendar prior to the actual date so you have time to prepare for it.

* * * *

Appendix: Special Free Bonuses

You can access your free bonuses here:

https://www.bizmove.com/bizgifts.htm

Here's what you get:

#1 How to Be a Good Manager and Leader; 120 Tips to improve your Leadership Skills (Leadership Video Guide).

Learn how to improve your leadership skills and become a better manager and leader. Here's how to be the boss people want to give 200 percent for. In this video you'll discover 120 powerful tips and strategies to motivate and inspire your people to bring out the best in them.

#2 Small Business Management: Essential Ingredients for Success (eBook Guide)

Discover scores of business management tricks, secrets and shortcuts. This Ebook guide does far more than impart knowledge - it inspires action.

#3 How to Manage Yourself for Success; 90 Tips to Better Manage Yourself and Your Time (Self Management Video Guide)

You are responsible for everything that happens in your life. Learn to accept total responsibility for yourself. If you don't manage yourself, then you are letting others have control of your life. In this video you'll discover 90 powerful tips and strategies to better manage yourself for success.

#4 80 Best Inspirational Quotes for Success (Motivational Video Guide)

For this video we scanned thousands of motivational and inspirational quotes to bring you this collection of the best 80 motivational quotes for success in life.

#5 Top 10 Habits to Adopt From Highly Successful People (Self Growth Video Guide)

In this video you'll discover the top 10 habits of highly successful people that you can adopt and achieve success in your life.

#6 Personal Branding: How to Make a Killer First Impression (Self Promotion Video Guide)

This video deals with personal branding. While promoting your personal brand, you'll discover in this video the ten most effective things you can do to make the best first impression possible.

#7 How to Advance Your Career 10 Times Faster (Career Advancement Video Guide)

The most important thing to remember about your career today is that you need to be responsible for your own future. In this video you'll discover 10 powerful strategies to advance your career faster.

#8 How to Get Success in Life; 10 Strategies to Attract the Life You Want (Self Actualization Video Guide)

To have more, we must be more of who we are. The secret is in the doing; none of it matters until we do something about it. In this video you'll discover 10 powerful strategies to attract the life you want.

#9 A Comprehensive Package of Business Tools

Here's a collection featuring dozens of business related templates, worksheets, forms, and plans; covering finance, starting a business, marketing, business planning, sales, and general management.

#10 People Management Skills: How to Deal with Difficult Employees (Managing People Video Guide)

Problem behavior on the part of employees can erupt for a variety of reasons. In this video you'll discover the top ten ideas for dealing with difficult employees.

* * * *

www.ingramcontent.com/pod-product-compliance
Lightning Source LLC
Chambersburg PA
CBHW070809220526
45466CB00002B/604